Identity Theft

By
Kennetta Morgan

Identity Theft

Copyright © 2022 by Kennetta Morgan

Printed in the United States of America

ISBN: 979-8-218-00021-9 (paperback)

Published by: Joseph's Ministry, LLC
www.josephsministryllc.com

Unless otherwise identified, Scripture quotations are from the King James Version. Copyright © 1982 by Thomas Nelson, Inc. Used by permission. All rights reserved.

Scripture quotations marked (NIV) are taken from the Holy Bible, New International Version®, NIV®. Copyright © 1973, 1978, 1984, 2011 by Biblica, Inc.™ Used by permission of Zondervan. All rights reserved worldwide. www.zondervan.com The "NIV" and "New International Version" are trademarks registered in the United States Patent and Trademark Office by Biblica, Inc.™

Scripture quotations marked (AMP) are taken from the Amplified Bible, Copyright © 2015 by The Lockman Foundation. Used by permission.

All rights reserved. This book or any portion thereof may not be reproduced or used in any manner whatsoever without the express written permission of the author except for the use of brief quotations in a book review.

TABLE OF CONTENTS

Introduction 5

Chapter 1: The Reveal 7

Chapter 2: The Blinders 15

Chapter 3: Identity Confusion 23

Chapter 4: Labels 29

Chapter 5: The Confession 37

Chapter 6: The Words I Speak 43

Chapter 7: The Overcomer 49

Chapter 8: The Conquer 53

About the Author 57

INTRODUCTION

In this book, you will recognize how the enemy has stolen your identity in various ways in your life. From your youth to your adulthood, he has used lies and the labels that have been placed on you by loved ones and people you trust to keep you captive with fear of moving forward or becoming your greatest potential.

As you begin to read this book, you will become more aware and awakened to how the enemy has blinded you and caused you to remain stagnant in different areas of your life by using your identity to keep you captive. I can honestly say that I had been tricked and bamboozled by the enemy several times, dealing with my identity and who I thought I was, and who God said I was. But, oh, how I thank God today for the inspiration He has given me to write this book just for you so you can be free the same way He has made me free from all judgments of man. I can assure you that if you read this book and complete it, your mind will be transformed with a new way of thinking, and you will be able to walk in the full confidence of God and who He says you are without fear of the lies of the enemy.

So, I encourage you to get this book today and start your new journey of transformation in your mental mindset, allow God to heal, deliver and set you free even in areas you didn't know you hurt in. Give yourself a new opportunity to live again in the fullness of life that God has given you, so open yourself to a life of freedom, go forth and experience new horizons in your confidence, declare that this is your year of growth and conquering the odds that had been against you. Remember that if God be for you who can be against you, Amen. God bless you.

Please share this book with a friend and help someone you know that has been dealing with their identity get free like you.

Jeremiah 1:5 (NIV) "I knew you before I formed you in your mother's womb. Before you were born I set you apart and appointed you as my prophet to the nations."

CHAPTER 1

The Reveal

In this chapter, you will be able to understand how the enemy has come into your life as a thief and how he comes only to steal, kill, and destroy your purpose. *John 10:10 NIV*

As I reflect on times in my life when I received a phone call from my bank alerting me that there may have been some type of fraudulent activity happening on my debit card and that I needed to call ASAP to confirm if I had made the charges took me to a place of how God consistently tries to alert us on how the enemy comes in fraudulent ways in our lives such as counterfeit relationships! You see, the enemy always seems to give us the counterfeit (fake) relationships first; understand that he knows our weaknesses, so those are often the areas he loves to target. Not to mention the people we love and trust and rely on, such as family and friends; he uses them to hurt us and delay our God-given purpose because he knows that they hold a special place in our hearts, but thank you, Jesus, for the

Reveal! We have been spiritually awakened. See, we often seem to allow the enemy to deceive us in our lives through people, situations, etc. But I declare right now in the Mighty Name of Jesus that all the blinders are being removed now!! And that you will begin to tap into a higher level of revelation in the spirit realm, Amen.

So, as I received the call from the fraud department, the banker preceded to ask me if I had made various charges on my card, and as I declined each charge, it really began to anger me that the enemy had violated my identity and had brought up false charges against me. That thief caused my credit card to be compromised and no longer good for use. I begin to realize this is the same tactic he uses in our lives to deceive us about who we are. He lies to us and confuses our God-given identity, but for some reason, we don't have a problem believing what the enemy has lied to us and said about us; we just claim the charges and pay the debts of depression and insecurities. My God! As you read this book, I pray that you will begin to see what God sees and what God says about you.

Psalm 139:14 (KJV) I am fearfully and wonderfully made; marvelous are His works.

So, when God designed you, He was doing something special, and how we know this is that we all have different fingerprints; even identical twins have a different fingerprint. So, with that being said, you are the original copy of who our creator made you to be.

Your identity has been successfully stolen from you when you began to live up to what the thief has lied and told you. Things like "You're not good enough," "You're not strong enough," "That's not for you," "Only certain people can have that," "You don't belong, you don't fit in," "You're not skinny enough," "You're not pretty enough," "You're not big enough," "You're too dark," "You're too light," "You're not smart enough," "You're too shy," "You're too quiet," "You're too loud," "You're not professional enough," "You can't start a business," "You will never be like them," "You should not even try," "You're not on that level, so give up now," "You're always going to be in this position," "You're never going to make it." Lies, lies, and more lies. The Bible says, in *John 8:44 (KJV), he is the father of lies*. Believe that! But on the contrary, you are just the opposite of what the liar has told you. I cancel every lying tongue and every lying spirit that has been sent out to frustrate your purpose. I call it null and voided, in Jesus' name. You will no longer be tormented by the lies that have been spoken over your life. I bind the delay of your God-given purpose and speak you back into position and possession of the plan God has created you to be and to operate in, Amen. Allow God to realign you. Glory to God.

Definitions:

Identity – the fact of being who or what a person or thing is.[1]

Theft – the action or crime of stealing.[2]

---

[1] Identity. (n.d.). In *Oxford Languages*. Retrieved May 18, 2022, from https://www.google.com/search?q=identity+meaning&oq=Identity+meaning&aqs=chrome.0.0i433i512j0i512l9.2248j1j15&sourceid=chrome&ie=UTF-8

[2] Theft. (n.d.). In *Oxford Languages*. Retrieved May 18, 2022, from https://www.google.com/search?q=Theft++meaning&sxsrf=ALiCzsaA_V4yLWxdRaUlFFFQrV3DfvR9eQ%3A1652923273615&ei=iZuFYqqZJbWHxc8P7bqDgAk&ved=0ahUKEwjqgcKEs-r3AhW1Q_EDHW3dAJAQ4dUDCA4&uact=5&oq=Theft++meaning&gs_lcp=Cgdnd3Mtd2l6EAMyDQgAELEDEJECEEYQ-QEyBAgAEEMyBAgAEEMyBAgAEEMyBggAEAcQHjIGCAAQBxAeMgYIABAHEB4yBggAEAcQHjIGCAAQBxAeMgYIABAHEB46BwgAEEcQsAM6CgguENQCELADEEM6BwgAELADEENKBAhGABGABKBAhGGABQzgdYzgdgxgpoAnABeACAAYoBiAGKAZIBAzAuMZgBAKABAqABAcgBCsABAQ&sclient=gws-wiz

REFLECTIONS

What has the thief stolen from you?
_____
_____
_____

How can you recover all that has been stolen from you?
_____
_____
_____

Do you trust what God said about you (yes or no)? Why?
_____
_____
_____

How can you learn to come into agreement with who God has created you to be?
_____
_____
_____

Can God count on you?

_____
_____
_____

Here's how you can begin to change the way you see yourself. First, start with verbally speaking to God, letting Him know that you will no longer fight against who He says you are and that you are ready to come into agreement with His plan to see your purpose for your life. Then write a small list of affirmations that the enemy has lied and deceived you into believing to be true about yourself. This will be the reversal of the lies Satan has told you.

Romans 4:17 NIV
"Calling things that which are not as though they were."

Examples:

1. I am who God says I am.

2. I am good enough.

3. I am an overcomer.

4. I can do all things through Christ that strengthens me.

5. I will pass this test.

PRAYER

Heavenly Father, I come to you today asking that you show me who I am in you. Lord, I now come into agreement with the purpose you have for my life. I thank you that I am who you say I am. I thank you, Lord, that I am an overcomer. I thank you that I am fearfully and wonderfully made in your sight. I thank you that I can do all things through Christ that strengthens me. God, I ask that you would help me to remove the blinders from my eyes that will prevent me from seeing the vision you have given me. Lord, help me to pass every test that you have allowed me to go through and to understand the purpose and plan that you have ordained over my life. I will no longer fight against your will for my life. I come into alignment and partnership with you. In Jesus' name, Amen.

YOUR THOUGHTS

CHAPTER 2

The Blinders

You will be able to identify the things the enemy has used to discourage you in your identity. Such as people, places, things.

As I grew up from a child to an adult, I recall different family members and friends telling me about certain things I couldn't do. I remember needing to be cultivated and not having someone concerned enough are knowledgeable enough are spiritual enough to see the purpose on my life, but God allowed me to be wise beyond my years. He allowed me to take other people's failures as a lesson to not go that route! I had to tell God, "Thank you for ordering my steps!" My my, as I pondered on my daughter telling me as an adult (twenty-one years old) that her first-grade teacher told all the other children their pictures were pretty but called her artwork ugly broke her little six-year-old spirit. If you could just imagine the pain I felt to come into the knowledge of this ridicule, oh, how I wish I could find that teacher today to serve her notice that God had a plan and a purpose for Nina. He has allowed her to become a certified Pre-K teacher where she is able to be an amazing artist and inspire her students in their arts and crafts! But I must say my heart has broken over and over with just the thought of abuse that children endure on a day-to-day basis from people that are supposed to love them. You see, I really believe that identity theft starts at a very young age when the enemy tries to steal your confidence and self-worth by using people we love and trust to betray us in ungodly ways, but God does not sleep nor slumber. As a seven-year-old girl, I remember my mom getting kicked out of my grandmother's house and having to go stay with my grandfather, who began to molest me when my mom would run errands by touching me in inappropriate places. It went on for a couple of weeks before I decided to tell my mom because I knew he should not be touching me in this way. They had a big fight, we moved out, and finally, we got our own apartment in South Baton Rouge, Louisiana, apartment 107. Man, I felt so free to not have to go through that abuse of my own grandad touching me the wrong way anymore. Hallelujah, Jesus saw me. When he passed away, I didn't even cry, but something in my heart wouldn't let me hate him. I actually felt sorry for him, sorry that this was the man he turned out to be, all because the enemy had also deceived him. See we must understand that hurt people hurt people and healed people heal people. Identity theft is real, so as I thought to my young self, thank you, Lord, I now have my own room. I just felt so liberated and free. I know that it was only God that protected my mind and body. Lord knows how far the abuse could have gone on if I had stayed silent. My God, break the silence, stop holding on to the pain you endured in your innocence, it was not your fault. I speak healing to your mind and heart right now in Jesus name, Amen. Break the silence will one day be a movement I will advocate to little children that are being abused by people they trust. They lie and tell kids not to say anything because it's their fault or things like they will hurt someone if they find out. God protect the little children and allow blinders to be removed from the parents eyes.

As I went on to live a life of purity until I was eighteen years of age, I didn't realize I was longing for love from a man because I felt that was the only thing that I was missing in my life. See, we don't always understand where these feelings derive from, but I now understand it was a seed of feeling unloved that had been planted due to the abuse and the fact that my mom raised me as a married single woman because her husband was in prison and my father was also married and living with his family in a different household. Although my father was always in my life, it was still different because He had his family that where in the same household being raised together. However, they always included me in family activities and family vacations. The only time I got to really be with them was in the summers when school was out, so imagine not being able to have your dad in the house with you building a bond and making fun memories that you would grow up and laugh about in your adulthood. So, I thought I knew what love was between age seventeen and eighteen. I hooked up with my daughter's father and decided that I didn't want to go to school any longer, so I dropped out. Eventually I became pregnant and had a baby at nineteen years of age, but God had a different plan. Thanks to God that I did finish school and became a stylist and worked in the childcare industry as God ordered my steps. So, here's where my journey began.

    I always knew God had a special calling on my life, but I didn't quite think I was worthy enough to walk in it because of the sin I was in. I clothed myself in rebellion due to fornication and my willful sin, but God never gave up on me. As I drew closer to Him, I began to feel a love that I had never experienced before, and boy, oh boy, did it feel good. Special thanks to my dad for bringing me to church every Wednesday night to Hearts of Fire, where I learned about the true unconditional love of God and it consumed me. Hearing about God was a constant reminder that He is always with you, He will never leave you and forsake you type of love. Thank you, Jesus, for the grace and mercy you have bestowed upon me.

A Few Key Things About the Love of God:

- God is waiting for you to come to Him
- God loves you unconditionally
- God's grace is sufficient for you
- God sees you

REFLECTIONS

So, I ask you today, what are some of the hurts, pains, and negative words you have endured are faced in your life that the enemy has used to keep you down?

_____
_____
_____
_____
_____
_____
_____
_____
_____

Examples:

1. Being told I'm not good enough.

2. Not having supporting family members.

3. Being abused as a child or by others.

4. Feeling I don't belong or the black sheep of the family.

5. Disliking myself.

6. Without a father or mother.

PRAYER

Heavenly Father, I just want to thank you for loving me and covering me with your love even when I didn't deserve it the most. Thank you, thank you, thank you. As I have gone through abuse with loved ones in relationships that were not healthy for me, times I felt like a fatherless child, you still kept me. Lord, I thank you that you kept me through the pain and heartache of life pressures, never letting me fall. You are an amazing God. You regulated my mind, you kept my body, and you're still the same yesterday, today, and forever more. Lord, help me to continue to see myself as you see me. I thank you for revealing to me who I am and for never leaving or forsaking me. Your grace is sufficient. I praise your holy name today in Jesus' name, Amen.

YOUR THOUGHTS

CHAPTER 3

Identity Confusion

In this chapter, you'll realize how the enemy will allow people you love and trust to abuse you in various ways that ultimately cause you to live a life of confusion about who you are and who you were created to be. As I stated before, I was molested by my grandfather, my maternal grandfather. I thank God today that it did not cause me to become confused about who God planned for me to be. You see, the enemy likes to use situations to confuse your God-given identity knowing that God doesn't make any mistakes because He knew us before we were in our mother's womb. So just to put it plainly, if you were born a female, he wanted you to be a female; if you were born a male, he wanted you to be a male, but the enemy uses the abuse of molestation, rape, prostitution drugs alcohol and all types of other horrible things to confuse your mindset to believe otherwise. So it's essential to renew your mind daily and cast down all wicked imaginations that exalt themselves in high places, which is your mindset. There is or has been a battle that you have been fighting every day to convince yourself that what you hear is a lie, but unfortunately, sometimes we believe it and act on it. But remember, the enemy is the father of lies, and he will continue to deceive you in these areas until you come to grips and understand that that's not who God said you are. Life and Death are in the power of your own tongue. Speak life.

A Few Key Points to Knowing Your Identity:

- You have a unique fingerprint because you were made differently from anyone else, on purpose
- Determine what is meaningful to you
- Discover your true passion and what drives you
- How can you make an impact in the lives of others
- Why are you trying to fit in when God wants you to be set apart (2 Timothy 2:21)

REFLECTIONS

Have you encountered identity confusion?
_____
_____
_____

What types of trauma have you experience through it?
_____
_____
_____

Do you want to know how to be free?
_____
_____
_____

Are you willing to do it God's way?
_____
_____
_____

Start by reading His word; it will reveal who you are.

PRAYER

Heavenly Father, I come to you today asking that you would help me to recognize who you say I am. Lord, I thank you that you will guide me through my identity confusion and double mindedness. I understand that what has happened to me was not my fault, so please help me to be able to lay it at your feet and forgive those that have disappointed and betrayed me. Help me to pray for my enemies and those who have despitefully used me. I want to be free from my childhood trauma and pain that I have carried into my adulthood. I thank you in advance for my healing and deliverance. I believe you can set me free from every curse and every lie in Jesus' name I pray, Amen.

YOUR THOUGHTS

CHAPTER 4

Labels

In this chapter, you will begin to reflect on times in your childhood when your parents, family members, friends, teachers, church family, and bullies labeled you. They may have said things like you're stupid, dumb, not smart enough, ugly, too dark, too light, too short, too tall, too fat, too skinny, you talk too much, you are a show off, you think you're all that, etc. All lies, but you found yourself carrying these labels with you through your adulthood and even still today.

I remember, when I was a little girl, I had fights with my cousin and fights in school with other kids because of what someone had said to me and about me. LOL that is why your mama is fat and ugly type of talk. Could surely start a fight, in my book. They say sticks and stones may break my bones, but words will never hurt. Well, that is the biggest lie the enemy has deceived us with because the words people use are actually the tool the enemy uses to break you. Just think, if you break the bones in your face, they will heal in a few weeks, but it takes years to heal your broken heart. Friends, we have to remember that our almighty God spoke the world into existence, and the Bible tells us that life and death are in the power of our own tongue (*Proverbs 18:21 NIV*). So everything we speak and allow to be spoken over us shapes us. So be intentional about what you say because it will manifest itself. There is a reason we should be slow to speak and quick to hear. *James 1:19 NIV* Begin to bind anything that has been spoken over your life that does not align with the will of God for your life, Amen. Cast down all wicked imaginations that exalt itself in high places. Amen.

Labels – I would often help around my grandmother's house when she asked me to do something, and in return, she would send me to the store and allow me to get a snack, lol, so you know I made sure to keep this going. She would say, "Nay Nay, come here," and I would say, "Yes, Mama, you need me to do something?" So because I would seem like the good girl, I would patronize my cousin with my good behavior, and she would call me a show-off, and in return, I would call her a messy box, so you know this name-calling would surely fuel a fight, and over the years, as I grew up, I've had other labels placed on me: "You talk too much," "You're too dark, "You think you're all that," etc. As I became an adult, I took notice that I was still trying to live beyond the labels that were place on me. I thought to myself, "Am I really a show-off? Am I an attention seeker? Do I really talk too much? Maybe I need to lighten my skin." I didn't realize those labels had stuck with me, but it was time to strip away all the labels that had been placed on me by man and to walk into what God had said about me. So, I began to take the labels that had been placed on me in a negative way and turn them into positive ones. I decided that I would punch the devil in the eye by becoming the very thing that he said that I couldn't, Hallelujah! Now today, I am a successful entrepreneur owning my own hair salon, Serenity Salon, a childcare center, Serenity Childcare Center, and I work for the department of education as a class observer. I am also a licensed insurance agent and own rental property. Now you tell me how important it was for me to be talkative. I had to open my big mouth and say what God had already spoken about me. So, you see, my entire career is based on communications, and I love building new relationships and rapport with people and families. I also noticed that the enemy would try to discourage you in the very thing God has blessed you in. Keep in mind, if you're told you talk too much, you might be a businesswoman or man, a doctor, lawyer or teacher. So, know that what the enemy meant for evil God will turn it around for you good. *Genesis 50:20 NIV* Be intentional about seeking God about what He says about you because what He thinks is the only thing that really matters, Amen.

REFLECTIONS

What are some of the labels that have been placed on you?

_____

_____

_____

Do you feel those labels have helped you or hurt you?

_____

_____

_____

Have you seen a label placed on you turn around for good rather than evil?

_____

_____

_____

How have you been able to overcome the labels that were placed on you? Is it still a struggle not to believe it?

_____

_____

_____

Decide – is this label the truth or is it a lie?

PRAYER

Heavenly Father, I thank you today for who you say I am. I ask that you will remove every lie that was spoken to me in my childhood, in my adulthood, and in my relationships. I pray that you will heal my mind and my thoughts to think on things that are rich and pure. *Philippians 4:8 NIV* Casting down every wicked imagination and every high thing that exalts itself against the knowledge of God into captivity (*2 Corinthians 10:5 NIV*), in Jesus' name, I pray, Amen.

YOUR THOUGHTS

CHAPTER 5

The Confession

In this chapter, we will begin to counsel with someone who can help us get free from our past hurts. *Proverbs 19:20 NIV* Seek wise counsel.

As I continued my journey, I realized talking to someone I trusted are didn't know about my situation had begun to help me to heal from the mistakes I made in my youth. (Confess your sin one to another that you may be healed). Seeking professional help, such as a counselor, is always a plus. The Bible says that there is safety in the multitude of counseling. It's a great way to get out things you feel inside that no one knows, and it will help you to begin to heal. *James 5:16 NIV* I began to see how the enemy would use generational curses to condemn the children of God, such as a history of drug use, alcohol addiction, pornography, prostitution, and the list just goes on and on. The enemy uses idols that are the strongholds to keep you bound, making you believe that this is it. Sadly, for me, it didn't matter how many times I went to the altar to repent for my sin, I found myself in that bed over and over again until God stepped in. I finally realized that this was not the life that God had purposed for me, but it was the very thing the enemy used to keep me bound because he recognizes your weaknesses. It always amazes me on how much you try to get it right and how much more the enemy will continue to tempt you with your own desires, yes, the desires you have in your own heart. So, let God be Lord over your life until you learn that this is not my desire, but it is the desire of the enemy, and he wants to steal, kill, and destroy my future. He will literally take your failures and turn them into shame if you let him. You must understand and know that God is a forgiving God, and He is faithful and full of grace. Let Him be the lover of your soul today; He's waiting on you. He wants you to live life to the fullest and to have it more abundantly (*John 10:10-12 NIV*), so trade Him today. He wants to give you beauty for ashes, the oil of joy for mourning, the garment of praise for the spirit of heaviness (*Isaiah 61:1-3 NIV*). Let him in today; He will give you peace that passeth all understanding that will guard your heart and mind (*Philippians 4:7 NIV*) Trust him today; He will lead you to the right people to talk to about your own life experiences to help you get free.

REFLECTIONS

Are you ready to break the silence from the hole that the enemy has put you in?

_____
_____
_____

Do you have someone you can counsel with? Or someone to hold you accountable?

_____
_____
_____

Are you ready to live a free and fulfilling life that God has promised you?

_____
_____
_____

What or who has stopped you from moving forward in your life, ministry, or business?

_____
_____
_____

Can you trust the plan and purpose God has spoken over your life?

_____
_____
_____
_____
_____
_____
_____
_____
_____
_____
_____
_____
_____
_____
_____
_____

PRAYER

God, I thank you this morning for giving me an opportunity to come to you boldly, to your throne of grace. Father, today, I break the silence and any hole that the enemy has had on me to keep me down. Today, I command the enemy to lose his hold off of me and my family now. I confess my sin one to another that I might be free, that I might be whole, that I may be delivered in Jesus' name. God, I thank you for another chance to get it right before you. Lord, I thank you, Father, that you allow me to walk in peace today as I declare freedom over my life. Lord, I thank you for the plans that you have for me to prosper and for me to elevate. I give you praise today in Jesus' name, Amen.

YOUR THOUGHTS

CHAPTER 6

The Words I Speak

In this chapter, you will begin to experience a boldness and freedom to speak life over yourself and every situation you face going forward as you denounce the lies of the enemy because he is the father of lies. *Proverbs 18:21 NIV* The tongue has the power of life and death.

As I journey through life, I have come to realize that I am what I say I am (*Proverbs 23:7 NIV* –as a man thinks it in his heart, so is he). I realize that I have been speaking defeat over myself, and that's why everything I spoke would show up, so friends, please understand how important it is to speak life and not death out of your mouth into the atmosphere. Be very careful about the words that come out of your mouth; they can either bless you or curse you because you are what you eat. (*Proverbs 18:21 NIV*) If you say "I can do it," then you can, and if you say "I can't do it," then you can't because you have conditioned in your heart and set your mind to believe that you are already defeated before you even try. So, try to not speak if it's not positive because the enemy is waiting on you to speak death over your life. That is his plan; he desires to have you and to sift you like wheat (*Luke 22:31-34 NIV*). He wants you to be defeated in every circumstance, but I declare today that I am somebody, that I am a child of the King, that I am an overcomer because He reigns, He rules, and He dominates my life. He is My God, and He is my Peace, Amen.

As you read through this book, I pray that you will get a revelation of who you are in God, that you will never be silenced again. That you will never be bound again, and that you will never be broken to the place where the enemy has a stronghold on your life again. I declare freedom over your life and family today. My friend, I speak to every shackle and every chain to be broken off you. I speak to every generational curse, any spirit of witchcraft to be destroyed now. Spirit of incest, sexual abuse, verbal or physical abuse, I command you to die now. I command any drug addiction and any addiction that controls you, be it destroyed now. The spirit of the lying tongue, spirit of infirmity, I command you to flee, in the mighty name of Jesus. Every yoke be destroyed and cast down, every evil thought to be taken into cavity and to the obedience of Christ, we cast down every thought and wicked imagination that exults itself in high places. You are who God has spoken You to be, and don't accept anything less.

REFLECTIONS

Are you speaking life or death over yourself?
_____
_____
_____

Do you believe that God wants you to live a prosperous life?
_____
_____
_____

Do you trust the process?
_____
_____
_____

How often do you pray and read your word?
_____
_____
_____

Do you have an accountability partner?

PRAYER

Most gracious Father, I come to you today thanking you for helping me to speak life over every circumstance. I thank you that I will count it all joy regardless of what it looks like. Help me to know that when I open up my mouth, miracles start breaking out because I have the authority that you have given me to speak life over myself and my family. Lord, I thank you that I trust you, and I trust the process, I know it will not always be easy, but I thank you for going with me and going before me. I thank you, Lord, that you would begin to send accountability partners in my life, that you will bring the new friendships of people that can pour into my life. I give you praise in advance for what you are about to do, in Jesus' name, Amen.

CHAPTER 7

The Overcomer

I pray by the time you reach this chapter, that you will have realized how Satan has used past mistakes to cripple you and shape your mind to keep you in a low place in your life. I pray that this has liberated you, that you are now free from the labels that have been placed on you, and you understand the tactics of the enemy, and you are no longer bound to his lies. God bless you.

I was truly inspired to write this book because as I looked around the world, I realized how Satan has a hold on God's people because they don't know who they are, and they have forfeited their positions of power and authority that God has given us. We have become subject to our imperfections and who the enemy has deceived us into believing we are, but today, God is saying a righteous man falls seven times, but he gets back up again (*Proverbs 24:16 NIV*). So just know that no matter what you have done, no matter what you have said, God is still a forgiving God, and He is married to the backslider (*Jeremiah 3:14 NIV*). So, know that God is waiting for you to return to Him. He never leaves us, we leave him, but thankfully, we can always go back to our Heavenly Father. I just want to thank you for reading this book. I pray that you were blessed, and that God has revealed your true identity to you, and if this book blessed you, help someone else get free by passing a copy to them. Life has its ups and downs, but He never said it would be easy. Identity Theft can really be traumatic in our life when we are trying to figure out who we are. Remember to speak encouraging words over every situation and no longer let the enemy steal your God-given identity. No one on this earth has the same fingerprint as you because God made you different, so understand why you're trying to fit in. God says He wants you to stand out. I pray this book blessed you and inspired you to change the way you see yourself as the way God sees you. Keep speaking life over your family and over yourself and know that God answers prayer and He is close to the brokenhearted.

REFLECTIONS

How do you feel after reading this book? Do you now understand your identity? And how?

PRAYER

Heavenly Father, I come to you thanking you for every person that reads this book that they will begin to realize what their identity is in you and how you knew them before they were even formed in their mothers' bellies. God, I thank you that they will receive a revelation of knowledge as they read your word, and this book will help to direct them back to you, and they will begin to speak life over their lives and identity. Help them to overcome obstacles and defeat and the traps the enemy has set for them. Satan, we cancel every assignment that you have set up to cause havoc in our lives. We cancel it and call it voided in the mighty name of Jesus, and no weapon formed against us shall prosper because we are more than conquerors in Christ Jesus. To God be the glory, and it is, so be blessed, God's beautiful children!

CHAPTER 8

The Conquer

In this chapter, you will be able to reflect on past victories you have won over the enemy and strategies that you have been able to use to overcome past defeats. Take out the time to write down situations nobody but God helped you through. Testimonies and victories.

REFLECTIONS

Have I changed my mind about what God says about me?
_____
_____
_____

Whose report will I believe?
_____
_____
_____

Count every victory.
_____
_____
_____

I'm not where I want to be, but I'm not where I used to be.
_____
_____
_____

If God be for me who can be against me.

I Win!!

PRAYER

◆━━━━━◆

Father, I thank you that I now have a different outlook on what you say about me. Help me to continue to believe your report. I trust you, Lord. I believe your word, and I thank you that I count it all joy rather I am going through trial or tribulation. I know that you are with me, and you are for me. I thank you, Lord, that I am not where I want to be, but I'm not where I used to be. Help me to continue to follow the calling that is on my life and order my steps that I may experience the blessings that you have in store for me. I know you will not withhold any good thing from me and that I will complete the good thing that you have started in me, in Jesus' name, Amen.

Ephesians 2:10 AMP

For we are His workmanship [His own master work, a work of art], created in Christ Jesus [reborn from above—spiritually transformed, renewed, ready to be used] for good works, which God prepared [for us] beforehand [taking paths which He set], so that we would walk in them [living the good life which He prearranged and made ready for us].

ABOUT THE AUTHOR

Kennetta Morgan is an entrepreneur and has several businesses that she owns and operates. She is the owner and director of Serenity Childcare, LLC. She also runs a successful salon as the owner and stylist of Serenity Salon Care, LLC with over 25 years of experience. Kennetta also owns real estate property and currently holds an insurance license as an agent in the state of Louisiana. Kennetta is the wife of Dr. Lawrence Morgan and a mother of five children and a GiGi of one beautiful grandson and one granddaughter on the way. In her profession, she loves to serve families and children in her community. Kennetta inspires her team to become their greatest potential with her positive, uplifting spirit. She aspires to help others to reach their goals, and if she's ever looking down, it's only to bring someone up. Kennetta is also a leader at her church, where she encourages others with the word of God.

www.ingramcontent.com/pod-product-compliance
Ingram Content Group UK Ltd.
Pitfield, Milton Keynes, MK11 3LW, UK
UKHW022219230426
12048UKWH00016BA/938